CAREER BOOK 2

16 Career-readiness Strategies
for Parents
of Middle School Students
With Special Needs

JIM HASSE

DEDICATION

To my brother, Bill,
who has shown me that a personal sense of adventure
doesn't have to wither with age.

CONTENTS

**Growing in
Self-confidence**

**Discovering
Disability's
Competitive
Advantage**

ACKNOWLEDGMENTS

A special thank you to Peter Altschul, Fernando Botelho, Earl Brancel, Judy Ettinger, Floyd Harris, Pam Hasse, Nan Hawthorne, Mary Krohn, Nancy O'Connell, Liz Seger, Ruth-Ellen Simmonds, Don Storhoff, Mårten Tegnestam and Bob Williams – all of whom (among many others) have provided me with valuable guidance during critical moments in my career development.

WHAT I BELIEVE

Over the last 20 years, I have identified a range of time-tested strategies I believe parents can use to prepare youngsters with disabilities for the world of work.

I believe guiding parents in implementing these strategies on a wide scale will bring these two results:

- More people with disabilities will be ready for work.
- Employers will find more job candidates with disabilities who they consider qualified for open jobs.

That's why I seek non-profit and corporate partners which have wide, established connections with parents who are looking for the answers I can provide about how to help their youngsters with special needs prepare for meaningful careers.

My message: I believe people can put disability to work as a competitive edge in today's job market.

For a long time, those of us dealing with disability employment issues have realized that individuals with a disability can add a valuable perspective to corporate efforts in the mainstream business world.

That message has had a difficult time getting public attention, but that may be changing.

I believe we can now more confidently state this finding: Employees with disabilities are more likely to bring drive, focus and innovation to the workplace than their non-disabled counterparts.

Consider the following three contemporary authors who have recently brought those three "advantages" of disability employment to the public's attention through books which have received good reviews in the mainstream media.

First, in "The Triple Package: What Really Determines Success" (2014), Amy Chua and Jed Rubenfeld discuss the reasons behind personal achievement.

Successful people, they say, tend to feel simultaneously inadequate and superior. They:

1. Believe they are, in some ways, exceptional.
2. Are insecure about their worth or place in society – that they're not "good enough."
3. Resist the temptation to give up instead of persevering in the face of difficult circumstances.

They may appear to have a chip on their shoulders because they have a need to prove themselves.

For those of us with a disability, for instance, we may have a personal need to prove to others that we are the "exception" to commonly held beliefs within our society about people with disabilities in general.

I believe that inadequate/superior package tends to generate a personal drive in "overachieving" individuals with a disability – a need to prove oneself by sacrificing present gratification in pursuit of future attainment.

I must confess that this inadequate/superior duality fits me to a tee. For a thorough examination of that duality in me, go to the directory for my series of seven Amazon books about my personal transformation stories as a person with cerebral palsy at cerebral-palsy-career-builders.com/transformation-stories.html.

Second, Geoff Colvin sums up the power of deliberate practice with a purpose in his book, "Talent Is Overrated: What Really Separates World-Class Performers from Everybody Else" (2010). He writes:

"...The most important effect of practice in great performers is that it takes them beyond -- or, more precisely, around – the limitations most of us think of as critical."

He pinpoints exactly why I believe it makes good business sense to hire people with disabilities who have developed the motivation to work hard at precisely the things they need to improve so they can contribute to a company's bottom line.

Colvin cites research that indicates what we think of as "innate talent" is more accurately termed "long-term, sustained practice at what really counts" driven by a passion to reach a goal (or in response to the triple package described above by Amy Chua and Jed Rubenfeld). In other words, Colvin says it's all about self-discipline no matter what the motivation.

Third, in "David and Goliath: Underdogs, Misfits and the Art of Battling Giants" (2013), Malcolm Gladwell offers a new interpretation of what it means to live well with a disability.

His main point: What is innovative, beautiful and important in the world often arises from what looks like suffering and adversity.

In other words, being an underdog can change people. "It can open doors and create opportunities and educate and enlighten and make possible what otherwise may seem unthinkable," Gladwell writes.

Gladwell even promotes the idea of a "desirable difficulty," such as dyslexia, a learning disability that causes much frustration for students as they learn how to read but, at the same time, forces them to compensate for that barrier by developing better listening and problem-solving skills – and by being innovative.

I encourage you, as a parent, to keep these considerations in mind as you help your youngster with special needs prepare for a meaningful job in an integrated work situation.

I researched and wrote the material for this book long before the afore-mentioned authors became popular. Over the last 20 years, I have gradually realized the importance of disability as the foundation for the resiliency of humankind throughout history.

However, only in the last five years have I publicly admitted that my disabilities, while they have made life tougher for me to live, have also, within certain contexts, become an aggregate advantage for me.

That reconciliation – and even love – of one's personal vulnerabilities perhaps come with age and the advantage of hindsight.

At any rate, please keep these initial remarks in mind as you review the following career-readiness strategies for your youngster. Your youngster's personal circumstances as well as the National Career Development Guidelines in the back of this book can also temper your thoughts.

Will your youngster be able to frame disability in such a way when he or she makes the transition from school to work that will help hiring managers recognize disability's competitive advantage?

Will those hiring managers seize the opportunity they have for boosting drive, focus and innovation in their workplaces by hiring your son or daughter?

I believe the answer to both of those questions can be "yes."

But, first things first. Your youngster needs to first grow in self-confidence.

STRATEGY 1 – LEARN WHAT SUCCESS MEANS FOR YOUR YOUNGSTER

Knowing when and why your youngster feels successful can have a far-reaching impact on his or her career down road in terms of finding fulfillment while at work.

For instance, I have found that defining what success means to me has helped me more easily pinpoint my accomplishments and identify the key success factors in my career.

That list of accomplishments and key success factors has given me the framework for developing my resume and my talking points for showing prospective employers how I can contribute to their continued success.

By first recognizing what must be present before I -- or others who work with me -- can feel successful, I have a bit of self-knowledge that enlightens everything from my career choice to how I supervise others.

If, for example, as a job seeker with a disability, I feel I need to have a perceived advantage over others to be attractive as an employee, this knowledge -- and the ability to use it -- can be my competitive edge in today's job market. In my eyes, making the most of that advantage is my definition of success.

Such issues, of course, are probably not much of a concern for your youngster at the moment. But, keep in mind the exercise below.

Ask yourself which of these four ways of defining success best describes your youngster as he or she participates in school activities.

The results of this quiz may give you some insight into which environments at school, at home, or at play can best support your youngster as self-confidence builders.

Defining Success

Individuals tend to define success in at least four ways:

Does your youngster seek recognition?

Being praise-motivated means it will be more difficult for your youngster to feel successful unless he or she receives some kind of external recognition for it.

Taking this too far can lead to self-doubt and being needy. Accepting good, healthy praise feels great for individuals within this group.

If your youngster is a recognition seeker, he or she should probably look for environments where his or her efforts will be perceptible to others.

This type of person will not enjoy utter isolation, must at least hear about his or her success and will not work well with people who criticize others constantly or ignore accomplishments altogether.

A praise-motivated person will never feel good about a job that he or she can't do well.

Is your youngster accomplishment motivated?

Being accomplishment-motivated means an individual will most likely feel the most successful when he or she knows a task has been completed and done well.

If you're accomplishment-motivated, though, one of the trickiest things is that, if you receive praise and you don't feel like you accomplished anything, you tend to think the person praising you is insincere and untrustworthy. If you don't see for yourself that a job is not well done, then you often feel you should have left it undone.

Does your youngster value of the feeling of "belonging?"

If your youngster is affiliation-motivated, he or she values being associated with a successful group. This loyalty could be to a family, a school, a club, a team, a nationality, country or even a continent.

At any rate, "success" is being a part of a successful group instead of being recognized for individual achievement.

Is your youngster influence motivated?

If your youngster is influence-motivated, that doesn't mean he or she wants to force someone else to do things "my way." Instead, your youngster wants to inspire others to take that path.

An influence-motivated person may feel he or she has a better way of doing something, a better plan for a project, a better idea for solving a problem or a better view of the consequences of a good or bad decision.

You can use the answers to the above questions as a rough guideline for how your youngster generally defines success for his or herself (recognition, accomplishment, belonging and influence). With that knowledge, you can:

- Help your youngster learn about what true success means for him or her.
- Guide your youngster in gaining the best fit for him or her at home, in school or at play.
- Help your youngster use that self-awareness (and the awareness of different approaches others may have) to work more effectively with family members and school mates as practice for future decision making in terms of choosing a career, a job, and an employer as well working with co-workers.

Just for the record, I tend to be accomplishment motivated. See how I reflect my definition of success in my completed online resume and how I tie my experience in learning how to live well with CP into my success in business.

STRATEGY 2 – USE FREE ASSESSMENT TEST FOR GUIDANCE

Here's a quick overview of the different types of free career assessment tests and how you may want to use them to guide your middle school student.

The Occupational Information Network (O*NET), sponsored by the U.S. Department of Labor, has a set of self-directed career exploration/assessment tools to help your youngster consider and plan career options, preparation, and transitions more effectively.

These career assessment tests, which are based on a "whole-person" concept, include:

- **O*NET** Ability Profiler
- **O*NET** Computerized Interest Profiler
- **O*NET** Work Importance Profiler

These instruments can help your youngster identify their work-related interests, what they consider important for working on the job, and their abilities so they can explore those occupations that relate most closely to those attributes.

There is no charge for completing them and obtaining the results online (or printing them out, completing them and sending them to your state workforce development department for a results report).

Users of these career assessment tests may link to the more than 950 occupations described by the O*NET database as well as to occupational information on CareerOneStop.org, a workforce assistance and information portal site administered by the U.S. Department of Labor and Employment and Training Administration.

As a result, individuals can make a seamless transition from assessing their interests, work values, and abilities to matching their job skills with the requirements of occupations in their local labor markets.

Your youngster has three options in most cases:

- **Take** these career assessment tests online.
- **Work** with a career counselor on an individual basis in taking them and evaluating their results.
- **Join** a group of individuals under the direction of an administrator who helps each person take and evaluate the assessments.

It may be wise to seek professional guidance, especially in matching your youngster's profile to the needs of the job market in your area -- someone who takes into account all aspects of individuality in the critical decision of choosing an occupation.

And, of course, since your youngster is still in middle school, you have some flexibility in choosing the right time for administering these career assessment tests.

O*NET Ability Profiler

This instrument is a career exploration tool that helps individuals plan their work lives. The O*NET Ability Profiler uses a paper and pencil format (the only one of these tests which cannot yet be taken online) with optional apparatus parts and computerized scoring.

Individuals can use the O*NET Ability Profiler results to:

- Identify their strengths and areas for which they might want to receive more training and education.
- Identify occupations that fit their strengths.

The O*NET Ability Profiler measures nine job-relevant abilities:

- Verbal Ability
- Arithmetic Reasoning
- Computation
- Spatial Ability
- Form Perception
- Clerical Perception
- Motor Coordination
- Finger Dexterity
- Manual Dexterity

Here are specific features for the O*NET Ability Profiler:

- The O*NET Ability Profiler must be administered by staff people who provide instructions to individuals taking the assessment.
- The User Guide is provided for workforce development professionals.
- The O*NET Ability Profiler offers flexible administration:

  1. It can be administered in individual or group settings.
  2. It has both paper and pencil and optional apparatus sections.

The O*NET Ability Profiler offers computerized scoring.

Results from the O*NET Ability Profiler:

- Are presented on computer-generated customized score reports.
- Can be linked to the over 950 occupations in O*NET Online.
- Are easily interpreted.
- Can be used on a stand-alone basis or with other O*NET Career Exploration Tools or with privately developed instruments.

The O*NET Ability Profiler was developed by experts who followed rigorous scientific procedures in the field of assessment research to ensure that it is a valid, user-friendly, assessment tool for career exploration, career planning, and career counseling.

O*NET Computerized Interest Profiler

The O*NET Computerized Interest Profiler is a career assessment test administered by computer. Users receive an accurate, reliable profile of their vocational interests that provides valuable self-knowledge about their vocational interests and fosters career awareness.

This instrument is a self-assessment career exploration tool that can help people discover the type of work activities and occupations that they would like and find exciting. Users identify and learn about broad interest areas most relevant to themselves.

The instrument is composed of 180 items describing work activities that represent a wide variety of occupations as well as a broad range of training levels. People can use their interest results to explore the world of work.

O*NET Work Importance Locator and Profiler

These instruments are self-assessment career assessment tests that allow users to pinpoint what is important to them in a job. They help people identify occupations that they may find satisfying based on the similarity between their work values (such as achievement, autonomy, and conditions of work) and the characteristics of the occupations.

The O*NET Work Importance Locator is a paper and pencil instrument, and the O*NET Work Importance Profiler is computerized. These alternative delivery modes increase the flexibility that programs and users have in career exploration.

Together, the O*NET Work Importance Locator and Profiler measure six types of work values:

- Achievement
- Independence
- Recognition
- Relationships
- Support
- Working Conditions

These are the strengths of the O*NET Work Importance Locator and O*NET Work Importance Profiler:

- Based on over 30 years of research by leading vocational psychologists.
- Extensive and thorough development effort. There was stakeholder input during all stages of development, which produced construct validity and reliability evidence.
- Extensively pilot tested; customer reactions overwhelmingly positive.
- Can be self-administered and self-interpreted.
- User Guide provided for workforce development professionals.
- Can be used on a stand-alone basis or with other O*NET Career Exploration Tools or with privately developed instruments.
- Results link directly to over 900 occupations in O*NET Online.
- Approximately 30-minute completion time.

Administered by computer, The O*NET Work Importance Profiler asks participants to indicate the importance to them of each work need -- in two different steps.

In Step 1, participants rank order 21 work need statements by comparing them to one another and ordering them according to their relative importance.

In Step 2, they rate those work needs by indicating whether or not the need is important independent of the other work need statements. Users receive a profile of their work values that:

- **Helps** them develop valuable self-knowledge about their work values.
- **Fosters** career awareness.
- **Provides** a window to the entire world of work via the 900+ occupations within O*NET Online.

Remember – you and your youngster can obtain each of these career assessment tests and individual results for each of them for free.

STRATEGY 3 – HARNESS HUMOR
FOR PUTTINGS THINGS IN A NEW LIGHT

In "A Spoonful of Humor," Dr. Stu Silverstein, a practicing pediatrician in Stamford, Conn., writes:

> "Laughter is a wonderful way to work off psychological stress. When we see the funny side of things, we shift our perspective. Putting things in a new light often leads to solutions to problems that we might not have figured out otherwise.
>
> "Also this may often be the best antidote to depression, anxiety, and feelings of hopelessness. One of the most effective non-medical treatments for depression is cognitive behavioral therapy, which actually helps chronically depressed patients to 'rethink' their old thought processes. This is exactly what humor does."

That "rethinking" de-mystifies what is often incomprehensible to us. James Thurber defined humor as "chaos, remembered in tranquility."

I prefer to think of that "chaos" as incongruity. "We delight," explains Dr. R. Dale Leichty, "in those people who can laugh at the incongruities in themselves and in the world around them."

Living with a disability is living with incongruity and collecting a series of inspirational stories, which are often more amusing than emotionally moving.

Freud recognized the humor in incongruity. He coined the expression "gallows humor" to explain the therapeutic effect of humor on individuals in difficult or life threatening situations.

The TV show M*A*S*H, for instance, showed that humor, both sophomoric and satiric, could co-exist in a health care environment and in a war zone. The doctors and nurses on M*A*S*H cared deeply about their patients, and laughter enabled them to retain their sanity in an environment that often did not make sense.

M*A*S*H is basically a series of inspirational stories.

How to Make the Best Use of Humor

I like George Bernard Shaw's philosophy about humor because it provides perspective for people who live with vulnerability. He wrote, "Life does not cease to be funny when people die no more than it ceases to be serious when people laugh."

A dorm mother, an English teacher and now an associate professor, Shirley Allen has the same philosophy. Asked about her life as a person who is deaf, Allen asserts, "Spending all of one's time adjusting doesn't leave much time for happiness. It's just not worth it."

Nick Peterson, Shaky Speaker Presentations, has a pleasing bite to his adjustment. Audiences marvel at his ability to speak clearly through the erratic movements generated by his Parkinson's.

Peterson likes to tell meeting planners, "I'm my own visual aid." As a result, he gets people's attention. They listen, and they remember his inspirational stories.

But adjusting to a disability doesn't come easy, and the humor involved doesn't have to be flippant. "For a portion of my life, I was angry because people we so quick to make assumptions about me," says Carol Leish, who holds a bachelor's degree in human development and a master's degree in education and counseling from Cal State San Bernardino. "But, through continued counseling and leading the in-service training, I've come to terms with my own abilities. I see myself as capable and other people as differently capable."

As Dr. Silverstein says, humor is a matter of perspective, and people who are living well with their disabilities have somehow managed (either through an inherited predisposition or a learned response) to see beyond their vulnerabilities and recognize as well as celebrate irony in those vulnerabilities.

And they often share their inspirational stories with others.

The Benefits of Humor on the Job

Victor Borge once said, "Laughter is the shortest distance between two people." Applying that observation to the world of work can become a powerful tool for your youngster with special needs.

Here's how Liz Seger, who has multiple disabilities and is a recognized expert about self-esteem (and can skillfully tell inspirational stories), handled a delicate situation:

> "When I was volunteering at the Red Cross, I had to go to a meeting of dignitaries for the city, but I'd slept in and dressed hurriedly and rushed to the meeting. I sat all through the meeting, left and came back to the office. As I walked through the office after hanging up my coat, I heard hysterical laughter coming from the branch manager's desk. I turned around and said, 'What?'

> "To which the branch manager said, 'Well, I knew you had horns, Liz, but I now see you've sprouted a tail.' The panty hose I had worn the day before had static cling to them and meshed with panty hose I had on -- and I'd dragged the both of them through the meeting without anyone saying anything to me until I got to the Red Cross office. I laughed.

> "I think that is the key to humor at work -- you have to be able to laugh at *your own* foibles first so that your co-workers or volunteers will see you think it's funny when you screw up. That way, they'll relax, too. Everyone, no matter whether you're blind or physically disabled or able-bodied screws up, and those screw ups can be a way of breaking down the barriers -- a commonality we all share.

> "My manager knew she could tease me about that. But the people at the meeting must have been uncomfortable about pointing out my 'tail' to me."

Stories Which Illustrate What to Do

At 42, Linda French developed epilepsy, broke her ankle and had to deal with severe arthritis. Within two years, she couldn't walk very well and began using a scooter. She tells about coming to terms with her new reality:

> "When I first started using the scooter..., I was very depressed. I felt very dependent on others and that strangers were all staring at me. I hung my head and avoided eye contact. This is very strange behavior for me because I am normally very outgoing, talkative, and make friends with just about anybody. I lost the job I had held for many years (and with it the rest of my self-confidence).

> "It took months of contemplation, but I recalled the lessons I taught my sons about doing everything the best you can. So, I gave my scooter a name -- "Harley" -- to ease the barrier and discomfort interviewers might have about it and found a job in short order! My outgoing self-confidence and sense of humor came back with naming my scooter -- and so did my employment.

> "That's what employers want: People who not only can do the job but also people who will fit in with other people (and be accepted by) the group. And, if you accept yourself, even with a little bit of humor about your disability, you will be accepted right away."

French's situation is one of my favorite inspirational stories because it illustrates how your youngster can use humor appropriately:

- She learned how to use humor in her own constructive way (a personal approach) to break down barriers.
- She used the right humor in the right time and in the right situation. She learned to be agile. She tempered humor she used according to the situation. She used her creativity to surprise people.

- She learned how to change her approach or avoid humor altogether, when someone is too uncomfortable to enjoy her humor.
- She gave others the permission to laugh by revealing the human side of herself.

I went through a process of acceptance similar to French's when I was a freshman in college and needed to push a grocery cart for stability and for transporting my books etc.

At first, I was extremely uncomfortable because the old grocery cart with squeaky wheels drew attention to my CP, and I wanted to hide. But, eventually, my grocery cart became the "cool thing" on campus, where students wanted rides and offered to lubricate the squeaky wheels routinely.

I believe Dr. Neil B. Shulman finds the right touch in using humor in his series of inspirational stories in "Humor and Medicine." He writes:

> "Life is the dash between two numbers on a tombstone. So we should try to make that dash as joyous and healthy for ourselves as possible -- as well as help everyone else's dash."

I urge you to help your middle school youngster develop a healthy sense of humor about the foibles of living with special needs. It helps make life (and working) more enjoyable and fulfilling.

STRATEGY 4 – RECOGNIZE
THE POWER OF FOCUSED PRACTICE

The key to success, more often than not, is simply deliberate, focused practice – not luck or innate talent.

Geoff Colvin sums up the power of deliberate practice with a purpose in his book, "Talent Is Overrated: What Really Separates World-Class Performers from Everybody Else" (Portfolio Trade, 2010). He writes:

> "...The most important effect of practice in great performers is that it takes them beyond -- or, more precisely, around -- the limitations most of us think of as critical."

He pinpoints exactly why it makes good business sense to hire people with disabilities who have developed the motivation to work hard at precisely the things they need to improve so they can contribute to a company's bottom line.

That's a "selling point" your middle school youngster needs to keep in mind as he or she prepares to eventually enter the job market. In fact, now's the time to help your youngster start keeping a diary of personal feelings generated by the need to practice due to a disability. Those personal-experience stories could eventually become very helpful as a job seeker.

Colvin cites research that indicates what we think of as "innate talent" is more accurately termed "long-term, sustained practice at what really counts" driven by a passion to reach a goal.

My Stories

My goal, from about sixth grade, has always been to be able to live an independent life. Even at age 12, I knew I could not expect to have a home and a family of my own without an education and a job.

I knew what the potential alternative was: living in a state institution after my parents died and my siblings had families of their own. Remember, this was the 1950s, and even my uncles openly discussed institutionalization as a fallback possibility for me someday.

I gradually learned how to turn my childhood shyness and fear into a positive motivation and self- discipline to live well with my disability. I took one step at a time. For example, I learned how to:

- **Live with a series of four house parents** during my grade school years so I could attend an orthopedic school 60 miles from my home farm. I would take the Greyhound bus to the school Monday mornings, stay with my house parents and then return home Friday afternoon.
- **Use a typewriter** (yes, before PCs) during grade school and use shorthand during high school so I could keep up with assignments.
- **Use the farm tractor lanes** in the fields of our home farm to learn how to increase my walking speed with crutches so I could navigate the hilly campus at the University of Wisconsin in Madison.
- **Become the photographer** for the in-house publications at Wisconsin Dairies by using the camera's tripod as a substitute for one of my crutches.
- **Obtain business, finance, management**, strategic planning, human resources and organizational development training to supplement my skills in journalism, public relations and advertising so I could become a more valuable member of senior management.

- **Build a team of five professionals** and delegate authority so others on my staff could gain a sense of fulfillment and carry out functions that I could not do as well due to my CP.

The anecdotes above show I had the motivation to work around obstacles through focused practice.

So, when I look back on my career now that I'm 71 and retired, there's no mystery about why I achieved my dream. I simply worked diligently to refine the skills I thought I needed at the time to help myself and others to do a good job.

I know people with all kinds of disabilities who have that same motivation and diligence. After all, there are many "over-achievers" with and without disabilities in this world. But, those attributes may not be as evident (or close to the surface) in individuals without a disability.

Self-discipline and Self-confidence

When the time comes to making the transition from school to work, your youngster's efforts in documenting self-discipline examples will likely give him or her the self-confidence that will be required to land a meaningful job.

At that point, your young person will be prepared to develop a job marketing campaign based on personal success stories which are based on examples of focused practice.

Such success stories, which can eventually be used in job interviews when appropriate, need to be short and succinct and honed for maximum impact on hiring managers.

Here's another example of a story from my personal experience that I could have used (but didn't) as a new job seeker just out of college:

> "When I was in seventh grade, I remember coming home from school and going up to my room at 4:00 each day to do the tongue exercises I had learned from my speech therapist. My goal was to be able to gain as much flexibility in my tongue as I could so my words would be more precise and people would more easily understand my speech.

"I don't know if my speech improved that much during my
middle school years, but I gained confidence and the ability to
relax during that sustained process (all with the
encouragement of my school teachers, therapists, my mom
and my weekly house parents)."

Help your middle school youngster develop self-discipline now
for doing long-term, sustained practice at what really counts in his or
her development.

I recommend you both keep a simple diary or journal of personal
thoughts about both "up" and "down" days -- material your future
job seeker can eventually tap for an effective job marketing
campaign.

STRATEGY 5 – UNDERSTAND THE IMPORTANCE OF WORK

I didn't give much thought to why people work until 16 years ago, when I was 55. Even then, it would probably have escaped my attention, if I had not been asked, during National Disability Employment Awareness Month, why having a job was important to me.

Here's what I wrote at that time.

10 Reasons Why Having a Job Is Important to Me

At birth, doctors said I would never walk or talk. Looking back on 34 years in business (10 of them at the vice presidential level), I now realize there are at least 10 reasons why work has been important to me as a person with a disability.

1. A job is the time-tested way to earn money.

Forget the entitlements, the lottery or a chance inheritance. I want more security than they offer, and the only way I know to make money, at least initially, is to work for it.

2. A job means I'm on the road to independence and self-support.

In most societies, working is a passport to independence, a luxury many people without disabilities may take for granted. But, self-support -- and the pride that goes with it -- is the real reason I want a job.

3. A job is the first step in solving some of my problems.

Earning an income and becoming independent gives me the opportunity to solve some of my problems -- disability-related and otherwise -- in my own way and under my own terms and within my own timetable.

4. A job gives me the means to create a better life for myself.

Addressing problems in my own way through independent living also means I have an opportunity to go beyond the basics of living -- which is part of the American dream.

5. A job is the best way to develop my work skills.

Part of the American dream is learning how to do a job. I did well in my first job (after lots of effort), and it became the foundation for my career.

6. A job means I have the possibility of getting a better job.

Getting my first job and doing well in it opened all kinds of possibilities for me. It meant that I could continue to grow as a person and as a jobholder.

7. A job gives me hope because my future begins to open up for me.

With personal and occupational growth comes hope, which helps me build my self-confidence.

8. A job is the primary path toward self-respect in our society.

With the self-confidence I gain by doing well in a job comes self-respect, an achievement I count as most important.

9. A job opens possibilities for purposeful -- instead of useless -- living.

Self-respect is one of the cornerstones of purposeful living, which I define as helping myself as well as serving others.

10. A job means I've taken a big step from exclusion to inclusion.

Inclusion, even in a limited way through work, is a big step for me. But there are always new barriers to overcome, so, for me, striving for inclusion is a lifelong commitment.

In writing that piece, I found approaching why people work from a disability perspective revealed how important employment is to us all. The need for self-respect and inclusion, both important motivators for doing well at work, is universal.

Yet, we are also all vulnerable at some level, and employment -- whether we're in business for ourselves or working for others – gives us the leverage to pull ourselves up to levels we could only imagine (and hope for) while in school.

I hope, at some point, my 10 reasons for why people work make sense for your middle school youngster. In my mind, these 10 reasons provide the rationale for eventually finding the motivation it takes to build a meaningful career when one of the obstacles involved is a disability

STRATEGY 6 –PLAN FOR A FUTURE SCHOOL-TO-WORK TRANSITION

It's not too soon for your middle school youngster to start thinking about how either the Ticket to Work or PASS program (or both) can help him or her successfully make the transition from school to work.

My Journey

As a 12-year-old, my immediate goal was to "go back home" to our "regular" local high school after spending seven years in orthopedic school in Madison, WI, 60 miles from our dairy farm.

I made it through high school, graduating second in my class and then earned a State of Wisconsin disability-assistance scholarship to attend what was then a state college in Platteville, WI.

Four years later, I graduated from the University of Wisconsin-Madison with a B.S. degree in journalism. There was no state department of vocational rehabilitation, no Ticket to Work and no or no PASS. I landed my first job where my uncle worked at the organization and the general manager of the company knew my mom.

In the last half of the 1990s when I was between jobs and trying to start my own business, Pam and I were living on savings and very little income. I remember our CPA asking us if I wanted to apply for

Social Security Disability Insurance. I said no. I didn't consider it a serious option at the time.

In 1996, I received a state enterprise grant to research the potential for training college students with disabilities about how to get hired upon graduation. The finding eventually led to the development of cerebral-palsy-career-builders.com.

Today, I would urge you and your middle school youngster to consider all of the available options for making the important transition from school to work. That includes exploring the potential in the incentives provided by Ticket to Work and PASS.

The programs

The goal of both the Ticket to Work program and the Plan for Achieving Self-Support (PASS) program is to help an individual reach a job goal and lessen (or even eliminate) dependence on disability cash payments.

The Ticket to Work program, implemented in 2002 and 2003, is a voucher-type program that is designed to provide job training and other assistance to SSI and Social Security Disability Insurance (SSDI) beneficiaries after they choose to work with an employment network (EN) or state vocational rehab agency.

Ticket to Work's goal to help a beneficiary get a job. After the beneficiary goes through the job program and finds a job, the EN will receive a monthly payment from Social Security for up to five years, if the beneficiary stays employed.

Available since 1974, PASS is a saving and spending plan (in writing) that allows Supplemental Security Income (SSI) beneficiaries to set aside their own income and/or resources, other than SSI money, for a specified time in order to acquire skills, services or items needed to achieve a work goal.

For example, people might set up a PASS account to save money for college, vocational rehabilitation training, a new business, a computer, child care or a personal attendant or job coach.

Beneficiaries may choose to participate in one or both programs simultaneously.

Under the Ticket program, both the participant and the EN must agree to and sign a work plan. PASS is tailored to the individual and has no time limits. It is self-directing. Participants decide what they want, what they need and how they are going to do it.

For Ticket holders, services for developing a resume, if necessary, will be handled by the EN. A PASS participant must prepare and submit resumes for employment three months before the PASS is supposed to end.

Eligibility

People who would like to participate in the Ticket to Work program:

- Must be age 18 to 64 and be eligible for disability payments.
- Must be in current pay status for monthly cash benefits.
- Must either have a permanent impairment or a non-permanent impairment that is expected to improve.
- And must have undergone at least one continuing disability review.

An individual can qualify to receive a PASS, if:

- She has a specified work or self-employment goal or is seeking vocational services for help in determining a work goal.
- She is between the ages of 15 and 65.
- She is currently receiving SSI or is eligible for SSI due to a disability.
- Or she will receive income (other than SSI) and/or resources to be set aside for a work goal.

Teenagers, at least age 15 but under age 18, may be eligible for PASS but not for Ticket to Work. They can use PASS money to earn a college education and acquire skills. Then, they can participate in the Ticket to Work program when they are eligible if they still need help in finding a job.

So, it's a good idea to keep these two programs in mind as your youngster moves through middle and high school. Knowing there are such programs available can be a confidence booster.

STRATEGY 7 – BECOME FAMILIAR WITH "JAN" AND "SOAR"

Increasingly, assistive technology devices are making impairments due to a disability largely irrelevant factors in how your youngster can perform in school, at home, and in future work.

The job Accommodation Network (JAN) is a service of the U.S. Department of Labor's Office of Disability Employment Policy. It offers an online Searchable Online Accommodation Resource (SOAR) system to let users explore various assistive technology devices for people with disabilities in educational settings and in work.

SOAR divides potential accommodations into four broad disability categories: cognitive/neurological impairments, deaf/hard of hearing impairments, motor impairments and visual impairments.

JAN also provides accommodation ideas for specific disabilities. See "Accommodation Ideas for Cerebral Palsy," for instance.

These accommodation ideas are not all inclusive, of course, because assistive technology is continually changing. If you do not find answers to your questions, please contact JAN directly.

Its staff of experienced consultants is ready to discuss specific assistive technology devices for your youngster with special needs in a confidential manner – a step which can build confidence within both of you about the possibility of "making it" someday in the mainstream job market.

STRATEGY 8 – PREPARE FOR TOMORROW'S TELECOMMUTING

New communication tools, such as "telepresence" robots, iPhones, iPads, cloud computing, and Skype, are creating an anywhere/anytime workplace.

That long-term trend has major implications for your middle school student who happens to have special needs. It means he or she will enter a job market 10 years from now that will have probably gone through transformations which make the term, "telecommuting," seem at least quaint and somewhat meaningless.

This is the major shift we're experiencing right now: Work is being taken to the worker instead of the worker being taken to the work. Increasingly, work can be performed in a formal office, at home, in a car, or on the bus. The meaning in the term "telecommuting" we had at the beginning of this century is evaporating.

"Telecommuting" was created in the either/or dichotomy of the 20th century when we still had strict distinctions between commuters and telecommuters, home and factory, family and community, and the personal and the professional.

It originally meant working at home by the use of an electronic linkup with a central office.

But, now we have not simply transferred what we did at our desk in the main office to our home. Instead, we've created businesses without boundaries that are highly focused on the individual performance of employees who are working everywhere all the time. Time away from work is now unusual.

Telecommuting Issues

This new "post-telecommuting" work environment raises some key issues which may or may not be settled by the time your youngster is ready to enter the job market. Here are a few he or she may face:

- **Balance.** How do you balance work and family life when your employer can call or e-mail you anytime and you are expected to answer in pronto fashion even though you may be having dinner with your family?
- **Accommodations.** Who pays for the accommodations you may need to do the work because you have special needs? Are you expected to provide your own accommodations just because you are working outside a company office or workspace?
- **Control.** Will your boss feel like he or she is losing flexibility for making changes in direction on a project? How will he know how much time you are spending on different tasks? How will she be able to have access to you and the documents you have? How will confidentiality be handled? How will drug testing be administered?
- **Insurance.** Who is liable when someone working at home is injured?
- **Evaluation.** How can work performance be fairly evaluated under work settings that are not standardized and, instead, are as varied as the personal lifestyle of each member of the work team?

In fact, that is what employers are currently most worried about: how to effectively manage a "virtual" workforce. It all boils down to trust -- that neither the employee nor the employer will take advantage of "off-premises" work arrangements.

So, as in the last century, reliability remains a key attribute employers seek in any job candidate, regardless of whether telecommuting is involved. That will most likely be the case a decade from now when your middle school student enters the job market.

Is your youngster showing signs of being reliable in school, social events and at home? If so, recognize those instances, specifically stating what he or she did that demonstrated reliability and personal responsibility. Follow that statement of fact with a sincere compliment about his or her positive behavior.

Due to difficulties with navigation, your youngster with special needs may eventually find telecommuting or "working from home" quite attractive, but you may need to make him or her aware of some of the negative aspects of telecommuting. Consider these factors. Your youngster:

- May have to supply your own tools and equipment -- not to mention workspace.
- May miss out on climbing the corporate ladder by rarely or never "being at the office."
- Will not have the discipline artificially imposed by the office.
- May start to resent the isolation. And this could lead gradually to depression.
- May find it difficult to draw a line between work and home and become a workaholic because the "office" is always there at home, even during the evening and on weekends.
- May find it inconvenient to be away from where the information, tools, supplies, postage and other work tools are stored.

My Experience with Telecommuting

Between 2000 and 2010, I personally put telecommuting to the test, after working 28 years in a corporate office.

I felt lost at first without the structure of "going and coming back" from the office each day, but I gradually established my own routine and harnessed my personal discipline to stick with it.

Living in a small town in Wisconsin, I'd get up at 6:00 each weekday morning and be at my home office desk and on my computer by 8:00 (all dressed and groomed) and usually signed off by 5:00 with a half hour for lunch and bathroom breaks.

As a full-time employee, I was the senior content provider for eSight Careers Network, a cross-disability online community for discussing disability employment issues founded by The Associated Bind, Inc.,

New York City, which was located six blocks from the World Trade Center.

From my home in Wisconsin, I worked with freelancers (all with some type of disability) located in New Jersey, Pennsylvania, Chicago, Seattle, and Ontario and Vancouver, Canada.

So, old-fashioned telecommuting does work. Its 2020 version could also offer employment possibilities for your middle school student with special needs.

STRATEGY 9 – MENTOR YOUR YOUNGSTER

People pop into our lives to influence our career development.

In fact, we all need a mentoring network of people who guide us (sometimes unknowingly) along the way in building a meaningful career in today's mainstream job market.

A mentor is any adult who guides the development of another person. He or she can provide your middle school youngster, for instance, with individualized feedback and guidance with specific tasks and adjustment issues in mind.

As a parent, friend or relative who has your youngster's best interests in mind in terms of a future vocation, you are his or her mentor.

A mentor does not necessarily just teach an individual about the importance of reaching a goal. He or she shows how that person can achieve it. For instance, you may need to help your youngster go beyond "how to do the task" to "how to work around the limitations imposed by special needs to be a skillful and reliable performer of that task."

A good mentor assesses all sides of a situation. He or she gives a mentee the freedom to grow at his or her own pace but always challenges that individual to test unchartered (and often uncomfortable) territory so progress is made toward a goal.

That may seem complicated, but please recognize that you can have an impact on your youngster without a lot of conscious effort.

So, cheer and support your middle school student with special needs in matters involving his or her Individual Education Plan (IEP), career exploration/selection, and all things leading up to the transition from school to work.

It's vital to have your youngster's active involvement in all things involving transition. This is what helps him or her become a confident and successful adult.

As a parent, you are now a part of your youngster's essential mentoring network, which will expand as he or she develops a meaningful career. Yes, it takes time and it is work, but it's worth it.

STRATEGY 10 – USE
STORIES AS A SHOWCASING MEDIUM

During job interviews, today's job seekers need to be prepared to reply succinctly to straight-forward questions about their experience as well as to take advantage of more creative approaches. For instance, they may be asked to:

- "Cite an example of when you felt you were illustrating your 'emotional intelligence' in a work setting."
- "Tell a story about yourself that illustrates your ability to build effective interpersonal relationships on the job."
- "Describe how you have successfully handled a difficult work situation that really presented you with a personal challenge. How did that situation change your perception of what you can accomplish? Why do you feel good about the outcome?"

Yuk, right? And, by the time your middle school student with special needs becomes a job seeker, who knows what the latest trend in job interviewing will be?

But, don't despair. Those types of questions give job seekers an unusual opportunity to showcase their true colors by telling short but powerful stories about themselves -- stories which can make them stand-out candidates who have acquired basic interpersonal communication skills.

Personal short stories which illustrate a job candidate's qualifications have always been powerful – and that will most likely still be the case 10 years from now when your youngster will be hitting the job market.

That may seem like a long way off, but the time to be thinking about how your youngster can practice basic storytelling is now.

Which stories are appropriate for a job interview? Think of the attributes most employers today seek in a job candidate. Here are six of the qualities I hear most often from the "wish list" of employers when they think of their "ideal" job candidate: *focus and stretch, perspective and communication, curiosity and creativity.*

That's your heads up for the need to role play with your youngster about how he or she would describe already-accumulated experience which matches what employers have always sought in job applicants.

Let's look at the six employer-preferred attributes I mention above and what they mean from an employer's perspective. That will give you clues about employer needs and the opportunities those needs present for showcasing your future job seeker's attributes through storytelling.

Focus and Stretch

Attribute Definitions

Focus is inhibiting your initial response to achieve a larger goal. Your youngster needs to determine (and pay attention to) what is important amid many distractions in today's complicated world. The ability to focus may be as important as intelligence in determining success in tomorrow's workplace.

Stretch is the willingness to take on challenges. Does your youngster see capabilities as fixed traits and, as a result, display a reluctance to undertake challenges that stretch them? Or, are abilities attributes that can be developed? Is your youngster proactive instead of reactive when difficulties arise?

Does your youngster feel adequate in terms of temperament and motivation to meet the demands, expectations and opportunities offered by others?

Perspective and Communication

Attribute Definitions

Is your youngster able to understand another's perspective, despite whether he or she ends up agreeing or disagreeing with that individual? If so, you may see the foundation forming in your youngster for knowing how to deal with conflict. That skill may also be helpful in seeing things as a customer would see them and understand what's going on in their minds.

In other words, is your youngster able to inhibit a personal point of view (listen first) to understand the viewpoints of others?

Curiosity and Creativity

Attribute Definitions

Is your youngster engaged in self-directed learning? Is he or she interested, curious and motivated by a certain topic?

Through curiosity, he or she may make connections between two or more divergent concepts or objects. That's the basis of creativity. Kathy Hirsh-Pasek, a professor of psychology at Temple University and the co-author of "Einstein Never Used Flashcards" and "A Mandate for Playful Learning in Preschool," says:

> "In a Google generation, where there are facts at your fingertips, the person who will later be your boss will be the person who can put those facts together in new and innovative and creative ways."

However, to be meaningfully creative, your youngster also needs to exercise critical thinking – to objectively evaluate his or her "new creation" in terms of usefulness, effectiveness, and practicality.

"Critical thinking is the ongoing search for valid and reliable knowledge to guide our beliefs and actions. Reflection results in and makes critical thinking possible," writes Ellen Galinsky in "Mind in the Making: The Seven Essential Life Skills Every Child Needs" (Harperstudio, 2010).

Here's an example of how curiosity drove my career:

It all started when, out of curiosity, I took a course about a "new communication tool" called the Internet at the University of Wisconsin-Madison in 1994. I remember sitting in that class and realizing I wanted to somehow use the Internet to provide an online gathering place for people with disabilities.

A good personal story describes the opportunity/challenge your youngster faced, how he or she was personally involved, and the concrete results of the initiative. From a job interviewer's perspective, that's basic interpersonal communication.

Here's an observation of Bernadette Martin, a personal brand strategist and author of "Storytelling about Your Brand Online and Offline" (Happy About, 2010).

> "The ability to tell a story about yourself is becoming increasingly important, both in person and online, as a key skill in not only getting hired but doing well in the workplace once you have landed a job."

Here's why storytelling is a key leadership skill. Martin says we retain 70 percent of our information from stories. Stories trigger our imagination and bring up visual images. Storytelling involves both the left and right sides of our brains.

Since an effective story can be so powerful in helping your youngster connect with people, Martin recommends that you guide your future job seeker in creating a set of five to seven very short stories about his or herself, each designed to resonate with a specific audience and demonstrate a specific skill.

I would add that one of those anecdotes can be an effective special needs story.

By developing this skill between middle school and college, your youngster is preparing to respond to future job interview questions designed to give employers a glimpse into why he or she should be the applicant they select.

It boils down to why your youngster is unique. Part of that uniqueness is disability. So what better way to illustrate that uniqueness than to develop a compelling disability story?

Martin says your youngster's disability story needs to have a beginning, middle and end, all tied together with a common theme. The story should briefly describe a situation, the action your youngster took to manage the situation and what he or she discovered as a result of that action.

In the process, your youngster needs to demonstrate his or her passion, values, goals, or strengths. A special needs story, after all, needs to show the listeners (eventually job interviewers) who your youngster really is.

In others words, each story needs to be a "proof of performance" anecdote: "Here's a challenge I faced, what I did about it, the results of my efforts and what I learned from it." Each is a snippet of your youngster's life.

Martin suggests your youngster may even include a quote from family, friends, or acquaintances about how he or she handled a situation, conflict, or challenge, which is always the "meat" of a good story. Those quoted can actually be "references" in the work world. Let them speak for your youngster at the conclusion of the story.

So, help your middle school student practice telling his or her success stories to family members and friends. Some of those stories may become powerful job marketing tools (and a competitive edge) 10 years from now, all stemming from communication skills honed in middle school.

STRATEGY 11 – KEEP CURRENT WITH CRUCIAL TECHNOLOGY

Learning 20 crucial technology skills now will help your middle school student be prepared for tomorrow's job market.

The first 19 of these crucial technology skills are part of an evaluation form developed for Global Career Development Facilitator (GCDF) training by the National Career Development Association (NCDA).

I added an additional skill geared toward online accessibility for individuals with disabilities.

Using a scale of 1 to 5 with 1 as "poor," 3 as "average" and 5 as "outstanding," I recommend employing the following list of technology skills as a tool to evaluate your own standing as a career-coaching parent and then comparing it your youngster's own self-appraisal.

_____ Basic computer skills (turning it on, using a mouse or keypad).

_____ Starting and using programs (menus, online helps, installing or upgrading applications, opening programs, saving and backing up, creating folders, clicks and double clicks, sending e-mails).

_____ Using a word processor or text editor to input text.

_____ Creating or opening PDF files.

_____ Creating a website (see wix.com).

___ Navigating the Internet and finding the information you want; opening multiple pages.

___ Knowledge of career-related sites and how to use them.

___ Knowledge of social networking sites and how to use them.

___ Evaluating online information on criteria such as relevance, currency, validity.

___ Chatting verbally online, using Skype, Google Hangouts etc.

___ Chatting using text-based chat.

___ Creating or moderating discussion boards or blogs.

___ Importing video and audio information.

___ Knowing where to find technical support.

___ Awareness of and following netiquette rules.

___ Knowledge of how to encrypt messages or files for security.

___ Running virus protections.

___ Saving or printing browser contents.

___ Trouble-shooting technological problems (onsite and from a distance).

___ Knowledge of online accessibility standards (W3C standards).

You may believe your middle school student is much more technologically savvy than you are, but instructors at the high school and college levels report that today's students may know what to do but don't necessarily understand the basic technological principles about how today's gadgets work.

Understanding "why" may be just as important as knowing "how" as we move deeper into technology during this second decade of the 21st Century. That could be your youngster's competitive edge in tomorrow's job market.

And, of course, this list of technological skills is not cast in stone. Help your middle school student add to it and modify it as technology changes so he or she will be up-to-date when it comes time to enter the job market. Make this list of skills a living document.

Remember -- it's not always important to be highly competent in each area. It may be sufficient enough just to know where to get expertise to carry out the particular function when it is needed.

So, in addition to updating this crucial technology list periodically, add links behind each competency that you find which can provide that expertise.

STRATEGY 12 – MAKE EXPLORING CAREERS A FUN EXERCISE

Your youngster doesn't have to learn from scratch how to choose a career. Our past experiences and the meaning we ascribe to them at the present moment often have a large influence on the decisions we make about our careers.

More specifically, careers turn out to be the result of a complex mix of life roles and the "DNA" *of those who came before us*, observes Judy Ettinger, Ph.D., L.P.C., from the Center on Education and Work (CEW) at the University of Wisconsin-Madison.

Genogram Development

During a CEW 2011 Summer Institute workshop, Ettinger introduced an exercise that uses "genograms" to help attendees trace the influence of their past patterns and current environment on their career decisions. She calls it "a narrative approach to career exploration."

She asked the workshop of career coaches and counselors to draw their family trees with a career perceptive in mind.

I drew mine -- with a box for myself at the bottom of a blank sheet of paper, individual boxes for my mother and father in the second, my grandparents on each side of my family on the third tier and finally my influential aunts, uncles, cousins and influential people outside my family in the top tier of the page.

In each of the boxes, I noted the individual's relationship to me, his or her particular career and the person's outstanding characteristics.

Genogram Exploration

Then, as I examined my genogram, I asked myself the following seven questions. Here's what I discovered while following Ettinger's exercise.

What did I learn about myself and my work as I examined my genogram?

My preoccupation with writing, even as a child, has become my occupation, and that was no happenstance. My grandfather on my mother's side was a blacksmith and didn't go beyond sixth grade in school.

Yet, he taught himself math and physics and made plowshares and shoed horses. He tinkered with the concept of a power lawn mower before it hit the consumer market. He wrote poetry and taught his new bride how to bake bread (and was known as the "fix-it" guy in his community).

My mother and father were the first to complete high school and obtain a post-secondary education in their rural area. She first became a school teacher and, instead of writing poetry (like her father), later wrote and published more than 1,000 "how-to" articles for magazines and newspapers such as the *Christian Science Monitor*.

I remember my mother coaching me outside the classroom when I was in seventh and eighth grade about how to write concise poetry and a strong essay.

What are my positive and negative memories about the past as a result of my genogram?

As a little boy, I had this urge to build. I would tell people I wanted to be carpenter -- to the wonderment of my grandmother on my father's side, who downplayed my dream because she knew it was unrealistic because I had CP and have difficulty walking and talking.

When I was about eight years old, I remember playing "preacher" in the backyard with my cousins. At the time, I had an uncle and great uncle on my father's side who were pastors, and we would take turns "preaching" in no-sense language we thought closely resembled what came across to us as children in their respective congregations as they spoke from the pulpit on Sunday mornings. I naively thought I could do a better job of communicating with the entire congregation than they did, even though my own speech was garbled due to my CP. In college, it occurred to me in a lighthearted discussion with one of my classmates that I may have been an architect in my former life.

I now realize my creativity also came from my father, who, as a farmer, was quite innovative. He invented a barn drier system for hay bales and was one of the first in his community to build contour strips around his farm's hillsides to prevent soil erosion.

What messages did I receive from my family about work roles and about choosing a career?

Everyone in my family worked. I even washed dishes in the kitchen as a six-year-old and baled hay while in college, even though I couldn't walk without crutches. But, I didn't understand why the kids in a family should have to help earn the family income (such as helping on the farm). During grade school, I lived with four different "week-day house parents" at separate times over a span of seven years in a city where I could receive daily physical therapy.

From those four families, I lived under a variety of work models (where the children didn't have to work because the parents were janitors, factory workers, school teachers, or people managers). I learned there was a life beyond farming and watched people outside my family learn how to choose a career.

Who are the key people in my life and why are they important to me?

My mom and her youngest brother taught me independence and provided the means for gaining that independence. In fact, my uncle put in a good word about me with his boss, and that's how I got my first job out of college.

From both, I learned the value of consistent practice with a purpose in mind and that the chief benefit of education was learning how to learn on your own -- two concepts which came in handy while I was learning how to choose a career.

In the light of my family, how do I define success and failure?

I believe success is finding my niche where I can effectively serve others and, as a result, find my sense of purpose. Failure is working with the goal of becoming best *in* the world instead of the best *for* the world.

Who in my family were most successful? Why?

My mother built a foundation of values for an extended family which has successfully made the transition from an agrarian tradition in which apprenticeship was the career builder to one in which formal education has given her grandchildren the opportunity to pursue a diverse set of careers: two thriving small business owners, a medical doctor, a soon-to-be lawyer, a priest, a process engineer, a surgeon and a renewable energy expert.

Who do you most want to be like?

My sister, first educated as a medical technologist but now manager of a pulp paper mill, reflects much of what my mother (and my grandmother on my mother's side) was all about in terms of acquiring "people skills" and building a life based on serving others. In switching fields of endeavor, she learned how to choose a career that was appropriate for her time and place.

I see my father's creativity and imagination in my two brothers, who used that agility to successfully navigate major structural shifts in forestry and in farming during their careers. Again, each learned how to choose a career that was viable amid changing circumstances.

Do you see why I became a corporate communication executive (my first career) and a disability employment writer (my second career)?

As a mentor, you can use this exercise (developing a personal genogram and using the seven questions above to explore it) to help your middle school student understand the dynamics of career exploration and why certain occupations may have some appeal.

That personal perception could prove to be a competitive edge in the job market 10 years from now.

STRATEGY 13 – LEARN
HOW TO CHALLENGE FALSE ASSUMPTIONS

Your youngster needs to start learning when to challenge personal assumptions about job seekers with disabilities – especially the three misconceptions below.

It's a form of personal preparation you can foster in your future job seeker by occasionally noting when these issues gain attention (sometimes negatively but often positively) in our public media.

I've found these three misconceptions seem to have a life of their own despite empirical data which shows they are false. These false assumptions are:

- **Job** applicants with disabilities lack business experience.

- **Employees** with disabilities accumulate more sick leave and have a greater turnover rate than the average employee.

- **Business** travel is not practical or needed for employees with disabilities.

Let's examine each of these three misconceptions.

I'll provide you with some problem-solving tools you can pass along to your middle school student when you believe the time is right – when he or she is ready to deal with the realities of these three disability employment issues.

There's no rush. These issues will always be with us -- issues savvy individuals with a disability will need to repeatedly address.

Lack of Business Experience

Many people with disabilities could very well possess extensive business experience, even though their resumes may look slim from a traditional-job perspective.

Take a closer look at their resumes. They may have been in business for themselves or have volunteered their time in for-profit and non-profit organizations.

More than four of 10 respondents to the first-ever national study of self-employed people with disabilities said they chose the entrepreneurial route because they "needed to create their own job." A similar number also said they had chosen self-employment with its flexible hours and working conditions "to accommodate a disability."

These are just two findings from a study conducted by the National Institute on Disability and Rehabilitation Research's Research & Training Center on Rural Rehabilitation Services, which is connected with the University of Montana-affiliated Rural Institute on Disabilities.

"Research has shown that there are nearly as many people with disabilities who own their own businesses as those who work for federal, state, and local governments combined," says Rural Institute research director Tom Seekins.

Volunteering is another avenue people with disabilities often use to gain business experience. Most motivated individuals with a disability will manage to land internships during college, but, upon graduation, internships are generally not available. Outside of "normal" employment, that leaves volunteering as one of the few avenues they have after college for developing their skills and proving themselves on the job.

After college, job candidates with disabilities also often endure long job searches or stretches between jobs.

Your middle school youngster needs to recognize these two problem-solving tools:

- **Some** individuals with a disability use volunteering as one of their job search strategies to widen their contacts with people who have varying experiences, backgrounds and lifestyles.

- **Others** volunteer so they can fill in chronological gaps in their resumes.

Greater Absenteeism and Turnover

A recent DePaul study of 314 employees across several industries indicates participants with disabilities had fewer scheduled absences than those without disabilities and that all participants had nearly identical job performance ratings.

Anecdotal and survey research indicate that employees with disabilities may be less likely to leave an employer than their non-disabled counterparts. For example, Hire Potential found that its placements stayed on the job an average of 50 percent longer than those without disabilities.

And Marriott employees hired through its Pathways to Independence Program experienced a six percent turnover rate versus the 52 percent turnover rate of the overall workforce. That's one my favorite problem-solving tools for addressing today's high employee turnover rate.

Remember, the costs of replacing employees, including those who acquire a disability, are high. The Employment Policy Foundation states total replacement costs add up to an average of $15,000 per employee. And many people today remain on the job just 23 to 24 months, according to the Bureau of Labor Statistics.

Business Travel Is Not Practical or Needed

At a job fair geared to job seekers with disabilities, David was rejected out of hand by a recruiter because his openings involved travel — and David has CP. The recruiter who spoke with David was conducting his search for qualified job candidates under a misconception.

People who have a disability travel all the time. There is absolutely no reason to assume that a person with a disability cannot travel for business purposes.

If a worker isn't given assignments that involve travel only because of her disability, she misses an opportunity to grow and (even more importantly) to demonstrate what she can do on the job.

Often business travel involves sales or persuasion in some way, and such success on the road can tangibly impact a company's bottom line. Networking done during business travel can bring an influx of new ideas, new tools, new intelligence and, potentially, new employees and new customers.

A business traveler is a goodwill ambassador as well as a scout. An achieving worker with a disability may miss out on such an important contribution. An employer is risking an opportunity by not sending its best persuaders – perhaps those with a slightly different perspective about product design or service delivery because they happen to have some form of disability.

Learning how to effectively frame each of these three disability employment issues at an early age will give your future job seeker the leverage he or she will need to do well in tomorrow's workplace.

STRATEGY 14 – DEVISE A PLAN
FOR OVERCOMING "STEM" OBSTACLES

Yes, STEM careers are hot right now.

But, I need to add a caveat. If your youngster has a mobility, visual, speech, or hearing disability and is intrigued by a STEM career -- one which uses knowledge of science, technology, electronics and math – he or she needs to be prepared to develop a plan for overcoming some of the obstacles that may present themselves.

However, most importantly, remember that these obstacles are not barriers that will prevent your youngster from realizing his or her aspirations. You and your youngster just need to be aware of them and develop a plan for how to work around them.

Graduates in STEM fields can find work as health care practitioners, teachers, farmers, top-level managers in the private or government sector, and even writers or artists.

In many cases, disabilities are not barriers in STEM fields, where mental capacity and creativity are keys to success. STEM jobs are often not physically demanding. STEM jobholders use their heads -- not their muscles.

The Barriers to STEM Careers

Nonetheless, in pursuing a STEM career, youngsters with special needs typically face unique challenges as they transition from middle school and high school to college and from college to employment.

For instance, your youngster might need special software or other technologies for following along in high school and college classes. He or she may need accessible work stations for lab classes. Or, your youngster may come up against teachers, faculty or employers who are fearful of dealing with a person with a disability.

Rory A. Cooper, Distinguished Professor and Chairman of the Department of Rehabilitation Science and Technology at the University of Pittsburgh's School of Health and Rehabilitation Sciences, knows about some of those obstacles first hand. Cooper has been in a wheelchair for 30 years after being hit by a truck while riding a bicycle.

In 2000, Cooper identified these three barriers to STEM careers for people with disabilities (and he's been creative in tackling them on several fronts since then):

- **Too few** students with disabilities are studying the physical sciences and math because, in part, they lack role models.

- **There still** remain some technical barriers to science education for high school students with disabilities. While many devices are available to compensate for various disabilities, some high school science equipment and laboratories are not yet accessible for students with disabilities.

- **Some people** still don't think individuals with a disability have the physical or communication abilities to work in STEM careers.

To overcome those barriers, Cooper has spearheaded the University of Pittsburgh's program to introduce middle and high school students with physical, visual, and hearing disabilities to STEM careers through job shadowing, robotic camps, and internships with local businesses.

Yet, a 2005 study by the Commission on Professionals in Science and Technology found that students with disabilities were more likely to choose computer/information sciences and less likely to choose the other STEM areas (science and math) at the undergraduate level.

By the way, here's another bit of career outlook information I find encouraging: The employment rate for scientists and engineers with disabilities is 83 percent, much better than the estimated 26 percent for the overall U.S. population with disabilities, according to the American Association for the Advancement of Science.

And, according to Nelse Grundvig, LMI Director, Wisconsin Department of Workforce Development, of the 167 occupations listed by O*Net as STEM careers, 57 do not require a four-year college degree.

So, pursuing a STEM career may be well worth the effort. If your youngster is so inclined, now is the time to "move to the front" by designing workarounds for the barriers to a STEM career.

STRATEGY 15 – FOLLOW NEW GUIDEPOSTS FOR CAREER DEVELOPMENT

Always keep yourself informed about the major paradigm shifts within the job market.

That's the advice V. Scott Solberg, Ph.D., Associate Dean for Research, Boston University School of Education, offered a group of Global Career Development Facilitators (GCDF) at a workshop on December 9, 2010.

I participated in Solberg's GCDF workshop about the old and new ways of managing a career during these new economic times. I was the only person in the group of 40 who had a disability, so let me try to convey his thoughts to you from a special needs perspective – career building information you may want to pass along to your youngster as the opportunity arises.

Solberg says there are now two new guideposts for developing a meaningful career in the new economy:

- **There** is always more to learn, and learning more makes an individual more employable.

- **Success** comes to those who are highly adaptable, resilient and proactive (three attributes I believe your future job seeker with special needs will need to highlight in his or her job marketing campaign because learning how to live well with a disability is a training ground for developing those qualities).

In other words, the key to managing future job uncertainty is to be open to -- and ready for -- emerging career opportunities.

We've undergone three paradigm shifts in career development, Solberg explains, during the last decade:

From a Niche to an Entrepreneurial Orientation

The old way:

We were urged to find the career that best matched our interests, skills and values.

The new way:

We now need to use an entrepreneurial approach --- one that recognizes that our employability is based on how well we assimilate career building information, recognize what is needed in the job market and hone a range of skills based on that personal assessment.

It's what we can bring to an organization (not our grades or aptitude or one specialized skill).

That means, over the next decade or so, your youngster must diversify his or her experience and accomplishments so they reflect a broad set of skills.

From Liberal Arts to Job-ready Education

The old way:

Four years of college were relatively inexpensive, a great way to expand our intellectual horizons and an opportunity for building a network for gaining access to higher paying jobs. But those four years did not necessarily make us job ready.

The new way:

Four years of college can be a debt trap, especially for middle-class students with few scholarship options. But college is still a prerequisite for gaining access to higher paying jobs.

And four years of college still won't necessarily make your youngster with special needs job ready. A two-year vocational or technical degree is job-ready focused and may be more economical in the long run because it could allow your son or daughter to join the job market sooner without heavy student loans to pay off.

From Seeking Promotion to Accessing Innovation

The old way:

Building a career meant keeping our jobs by doing good work and doing well enough to get promoted.

The new way:

Building a career comes from diversifying our skills and maintaining access to the latest innovations in technology and in communication as well as in the shifts of what are considered the best practices within our profession.

Resiliency Is the Key

So, the most important bit of career building information here is that your youngster, as he or she develops a career focus, must learn how to handle the uncertainty and stress that characterize the 21st century business environment and be resilient in the workplace.

In more concise terms, your youngster must harness the anger and depression he or she may sometimes experience due to the uncertainty and stress that everyone is experiencing as well as the anxiety and lack of self-confidence he or she may feel as a job seeker with special needs and channel it into purposeful action and practice.

But let's not forget the bit of career building information that is good news for your youngster. As an accomplishing individual with special needs, your middle school student may be already acquiring the attributes tomorrow's employers will need – precisely the lessons he or she is learning by addressing (and working around) the roadblocks disability tends to throw in the way of navigating everyday life.

Consider what the contemporary work environment requires of employees. It'll likely be even more stringent during the third decade of the 21st Century, according to Solberg. Your middle school youngster needs to start preparing now for eventually answering this series of potential issues.

Life-long learning

What proof do you have that you're committed to keeping up-to-date with new developments within your field or profession and with today's continually evolving methods of communication and collaboration?

Resiliency

What personal stories do you have which can show hiring managers that you've learned how to be resilient by dealing effectively with your disability? How have you transferred your personal resiliency to a work situation (either for pay or as a volunteer)?

Entrepreneurship

How can you show hiring managers that you're passionate about your work, that you think in terms of possibilities instead of pitfalls, that you're adaptable in difficult circumstances, that you're a motivator for those who are around you, and that you're determined to succeed in what counts? This the entrepreneurial spirit today's employers seek in job candidates.

Job readiness

If you feel you're not job ready for a specific position, are you willing to volunteer your time at that company to gain the needed experience?

Innovation

How can you transfer to a work situation what you've learned about working around challenges due to your disability?

Purposeful action and practice

What has your time in rehab taught you about sticking with a routine schedule to achieve a goal, even though it may be boring, unpleasant or painful?

This is the type of career building information I wish I had when I was 14 – a roadmap for getting ready for work (even though full-time employment may be more than a decade away). But there's no rush. Your youngster has plenty of time to develop his or her own base of career building information and reflect on what it all means in personal terms. The time to start, however, is now.

That's why I believe it's important for your youngster to do two things: Follow career-building trends online and keep a journal about his or her personal struggles and triumphs of living with special needs (which will eventually be a rich resource of success stories to share with prospective employers).

STRATEGY 16 – PREPARE
FOR THE QUESTION NOT ASKED

The question your middle school student will most likely face when he or she enters tomorrow's world of work is this:

"You have a disability. Why should I hire you?"

That question, of course, will probably not be asked at all. If it is, it will be so indirect that your youngster will need to be quite perceptive in determining what is unasked but needs answering.

Over the years, I have collected insights from others within the disability community which I believe are viable answers to that unasked question. Those answers can be boiled down to two concepts: tenacity and innovation.

Tenacity Learned Through Patience and Perseverance

Job candidates who can show they have developed patience through struggle in addressing their vulnerabilities can be prime applicants because they'll likely help an employer reduce employee turnover and increase productivity. That's one of my favorite answers.

Business managers will be able to get a jump on competitors by tapping your youngster's motivation – that personal drive honed by personal necessary you probably see in your youngster on a daily basis.

Smart employers will recognize that personal drive as a competitive edge they need to continue their success because your youngster will most likely stick with them through good times and bad. Those smart employers will also realize that your youngster will need an opportunity for on-the-job autonomy and personal growth under an umbrella of a compelling corporate vision – the essential ingredients for low employee turnover.

Many employees today remain on the job for about 23 to 24 months, according to the U.S. Bureau of Labor Statistics.

Why?

The social contract between employer and employee is long gone. That social contract said, in essence: "Stick with me as your employer, and I'll take care of you. I'll train you and promote you to positions of higher authority when you prove that you've used that training to make yourself qualified for those positions. As part of this agreement, I'll compensate you fairly in terms of salary, bonuses, pensions etc."

Today employees are mostly on their own. They're personally responsible for their own career development and their retirement planning. And, they may have sizable debt accumulated over the years they spent gaining an education.

They job hop because they assume that's the quickest way to "get ahead," gain more responsibility and pay off their student loans, buy a home, raise a family etc.

Besides, they find today's jobs in many sectors offer little challenge. Those jobs are well defined, can be learned fairly quickly and soon become routine – offering little opportunity for real learning. Learning, after all, stops when a task becomes routine.

So, today's workplace is generally set up to encourage effective employees to "move on." After all, today's young people have spent 20 or more years in a "learning environment," and now, all of a sudden, they feel that their learning has stopped. They get bored with routine.

I have personally experienced that frustration, but, as a person with CP, I'm also continually challenged simply due to my physical circumstances.

Walking, for instance, is always a conscious effort for me because I know one misstep, particularly on wet tile or on an uneven sidewalk, can mean I'll fall, gash up my knuckles etc.

That's why I buy special non-skid tips for my crutches. That's why I recently found and bought a light-weight electric scooter that I can carry in the trunk of our car and skip the crutches altogether when Pam and I go to the shopping mall. The lithium battery only weighs two pounds and saves a lot of hefty lifting (the battery on my older scooter weighs 19 pounds).

In short, I catch myself always looking ahead, anticipating what could happen – even in my work. I don't mind mundane work because I see the big picture.

I've gone through the rehab routine – lots of purposeful (and often lonely) practice that is always tough but sometimes shows results and means a better life for me.

Learning how to live just a little bit better with my CP takes time and energy. Maybe that's why I don't get bored very often. I stick with a task because, in various ways, it's always new to me in the sense that it's not routine and offers the challenge (and potential outcome) I need.

In conversations with your middle school youngster, find opportunities to check if this "perseverance" concept is one of the answers which ring true for him or her and which could potentially be the cornerstone of a future job marketing campaign.

Innovation Honed Through Problem-solving Ability

Personal necessity has driven my success in business and, fortunately, I've worked in businesses which have allowed me to transfer my personal problem solving skills to workplace challenges.

You'll find that orientation in many job candidates with disabilities, who have developed the habit of continually stretching themselves so they can live a little bit better with their vulnerabilities.

People who know how to use their own best judgment are one of the keys to innovation (and success) in the 21st Century.

That was even true in 1956. My physical therapist was reluctant to recommend crutches for me because she thought I would become too dependent on them and that they would prevent me from learning how to walk independently without them. I had my doubts about her reluctance, and that doubt turned out to be helpful for me.

In 1962, I did some research and went out and bought some Canadian-style crutches myself (all before the Internet) because through high school and my first two years of college I found myself hugging the walls for stability and unable to cross streets safely without an "arm" from someone else.

At 71, I now have successfully developed a four-stage mobility strategy that works for me – all without the help of a state or private agency. I have my Fetterman forearm crutches (always in our car), my TravelScoot scooter in the trunk of our car, my Amigo scooter for getting around downtown Madison and my Invacare walker, which I use in our condo.

During the 1970s, I learned to transfer my personal problem solving ability to matters on the job. As a company editor and photographer, for instance, I saw an opportunity to dramatize our company's entry into the whey processing business through unusual camera angles.

One day (before the advent of OSHA), I climbed 30 feet to a cat walk above the company's new whey evaporator to capture a photo which emphasized the complexity of the just-finished stainless steel network.

I did it by leaving my crutches on the ground level and slowly climbing the cat walk's stairs, using the railing and my camera's tripod for stability.

I knew I could do it, and I captured photos I used in various publications for the following two years. But, at the time, I could see a mixture of doubt, fear and puzzlement in the faces of the workers as they watched me slowly carry out what I considered just another part of my job.

Now that I look back on that incident, I feel lucky to have worked within a company culture which was not hobbled by a spider web of internal rules and regulations. As employees, we generally understood that we were expected to use our own best judgment in performing our job tasks – even though we were bound to make mistakes sometimes, face the consequences and maybe retrace some steps to correct a situation.

I was engaged in helping the company be the best it could be because I knew we were all engaged in serving our dairy farmer members. I felt I had autonomy in carrying out the duties of my job, and I had an opportunity to develop my skills on the job.

Under that environment, I had an opportunity 20 years later to direct a company-wide communication audit during the early 1990s as the organization's vice president for corporate communication.

My CEO had doubts about the usefulness of the audit, but he approved it and we found, through the results of audit, the steps we needed to take to improve communication at specific levels within the organization and at specific locations.

A corporate climate which fosters employee autonomy and personal growth under an umbrella of a compelling vision can be, at times, risky and sometimes messy but also rewarding. It can spawn innovation.

The company survived 30 years of major dairy industry reorganization through merger and consolidation, mainly, I think, because it was innovative. We could get things done.

And, in a way, I became an example of that "can do" spirit. My work became one of those answers to the question, "Why is this guy working here?" – a query that could rightly come from those not familiar with "our" company situation, where vulnerability and ambiguity were not only tolerated but embraced.

Tenacity and innovation: Those are two quick-but-powerful answers your future jobseeker with special needs can use when replying to an employer's inevitable question, "Why should I hire you?"

SUMMARY

Preparing for a meaningful career as a middle school student with special needs can seem overwhelming at times. But, as a career-coaching parent, you can help your youngster to do just that by focusing on these key strategies:

Growing in Self-confidence

Strategy 1: Learn What Success Means for Your Youngster - Knowing when and why your youngster feels successful can have a far-reaching impact on his or her career down road in terms of finding fulfillment while at work.

Strategy 2: Use Free Assessment Tests for Guidance – O*NET can help youngsters identify their work-related interests, what they consider important for working on the job, and their abilities so they can explore those occupations that relate most closely to those attributes.

Strategy 3: Harness Humor for Putting Things in a New Light - Help your youngster develop a healthy sense of humor about the foibles of living with special needs. It helps make life (and working) more enjoyable and fulfilling.

Strategy 4: Recognize the Power of Focused Practice - The key to success, more often than not, is simply deliberate, focused practice – not luck or innate talent.

Strategy 5: Understand the Importance of Work - The need for self-respect and inclusion, both important motivators for doing well at work, is universal. It provides the rationale for eventually finding the motivation it takes to build a meaningful career when one of the obstacles involved is a disability.

Strategy 6: Plan for a Future School-to-work Transition - It's not too soon for your middle school youngster to start thinking about how either the Ticket to Work or PASS program (or both) can help him or her successfully make the transition from school to work.

Strategy 7: Become Familiar with JAN and SOAR - Increasingly, assistive technology devices are making impairments due to disability largely irrelevant factors in how your youngster can perform in school, at home, and in future work.

Strategy 8: Prepare for Tomorrow's Telecommuting - Old-fashioned telecommuting does work. Its 2020 version could offer employment possibilities for your middle school student.

Strategy 9: Mentor Your Youngster - As a parent, you are now a part of your youngster's essential mentoring network, which will expand as he or she develops a meaningful career.

Discovering Disability's Competitive Advantage

Strategy 10: Use Stories as a Showcasing Medium - Help your middle school student practice telling his or her success stories to family members and friends. Some of those stories may become powerful job marketing tools (and a competitive edge) 10 years from now, all stemming from communication skills honed in middle school.

Strategy 11: Keep Current with Crucial Technology - Learning 20 crucial technology skills now will help your middle school student be prepared for tomorrow's job market.

Strategy 12: Make Exploring Careers a Fun Exercise – Developing and discussing a personal genogram can help your middle school student understand the dynamics of career exploration and why certain occupations may seem appealing.

Strategy 13: Learn How to Challenge False Assumptions - Learning how to effectively frame three key disability employment issues at an early age will give your future job seeker the leverage he or she will need to do well in tomorrow's workplace.

Strategy 14: Plan for Overcoming STEM Obstacles - Pursuing a STEM career may be well worth the effort. If your youngster is so inclined, now is the time to "move to the front" by designing workarounds for the barriers to a STEM career.

Strategy 15: Follow New Guideposts for Career Development - It's important for your youngster to do two things: Fellow career-building trends online and keep a journal about his or her personal struggles and triumphs of living with special needs (which will eventually be a rich resource of success stories to share with prospective employers).

Strategy 16: Prepare for the Question Not Asked - Tenacity and innovation: Those are two quick-but-powerful answers your future job seeker with special needs can use when replying to an employer's inevitable question, "Why should I hire you?"

I wish you much success in working with your new job finder on these 16 key career-building strategies.

NATIONAL CAREER DEVELOPMENT GUIDELINES

According to the National Career Development Guidelines (NCDG), here is what your youngster should be able to do during middle school:

- *Recognize* that understanding one's personal interests, likes, and dislikes is a step toward building and maintaining a positive **self-concept**.

- *Identify* respect for **diversity** as an essential positive interpersonal skill.

- *Recognize* that **growth** and change are essential parts of career development.

- *Affirm* the need for **balance** among personal, leisure, community, learner, family and work roles.

- *Recognize* that **educational** achievement and performance levels are needed to reach personal and career goals.

- *Realize* that ongoing, **lifetime** learning enhances one's ability to function well in a diverse and changing economy.

- *Describe* why creating and managing a **career plan** is essential to meeting career goals.

- *Describe* the process of making **decisions** as one key aspect of career management.

- *Recognize* the importance of accurate, current and unbiased career **information** in planning and managing one's career.

- *Recognize* the variety of **skills** (such as communicating, critical thinking, and problem solving) that are important for success and advancement in school and work.

- *Realize* that **changing employment trends**, societal needs and economic conditions have an impact on one's career path.

LAST THOUGHTS

If they would have known, my college classmates would have said that, after graduation in 1965, I ended up working in the "armpit of Wisconsin," a crossroads with a total population of 187 people who supported three bars and two churches.

But, my story about how I became a vice president for a Fortune 500 company in the 1980s is essentially a narrative about the three attributes I discovered among my coworkers in that tiny town: acceptance, patience and inclusion.

Those characteristics were not mandated by law. After all, the Americans with Disabilities Act (ADA) didn't become law until 1990.

But, three decades ago, in the rural Midwest, those values were not uncommon.

In my case, I started working in my first job out of college for a local dairy cooperative. It was 1965. I had grown up on a dairy farm, worked on 4-H projects, went to a small high school and attended church on Sunday mornings. Most of my coworkers had a similar background.

In 1965, what made me different from my coworkers is that I had a college education and I had CP. Yes, I stuck out as unusual, but that didn't seem to matter much because I was a "farm boy," the general manager of the cooperative (Floyd) knew my family as neighbors, my uncle (Dean) was the cooperative's chief engineer and my boss (Bob) had gone to college with a classmate who also had CP.

As a commodity-focused business which valued financial stability, tangible results and equal treatment for the owners (the farmers who supplied the milk for butter and cheese manufacturing), the cooperative experienced tremendous growth between 1965 and 1995 as the Midwest dairy industry restructured through many mergers and consolidations of local cooperative and privately-owned cheese manufacturing plants.

Automation and technology drove that restructuring. Yet, in 1979, when I became a member of the organization's senior management team, I realized we still basically consisted of grownup "farm boys" who went to Friday-night football games, attended the same churches and preferred buttered crackers as a hors d'oeuvre.

The organization's core values survived the restructuring, allowing me to find my own bearings and prove what I could do within that corporate culture.

As a 71-year-old, I now believe we almost always learn something from each work experience – even in so-called "rotten" jobs, a term I didn't hear very often in the 1960s, which compared to today's sluggish job market, were "pretty good" years.

After graduating from college, my first job was writing and editing "copy." My "desk" was a foldable (and wobbly) card table in the back of the dingy break room where I had all-day access to the coffee pot and an electric "milk house heater." I was routinely interrupted by co-workers who were ready for a 15-minute "party."

Many days I was discouraged because I felt caught in a "dead-end" job (and disliked coffee). But I also honed my writing and copy editing skills and learned newsletter layout during those first two years in the break room. It was not a "rotten" job." I now know it was a job which provided the experience I needed.

Even then, I knew it was another small step in my personal quest to build an independent life, admitting that there would likely be many roadblocks to achieving that dream because of CP. I knew, despite the disappointment (I had dreamed about working on Wacker Drive in Chicago as a new college grad) and unpleasantness, that job would eventually be my passport to a meaningful career.

And it did. 20 years later, I ended up as vice president for corporate communication for that same company (now Foremost Farms USA), a position I held for 10 years.

ABOUT JIM HASSE, THE AUTHOR

Jim Hasse is the founder of <u>cerebral-palsy-career-builders.com</u>, the comprehensive career coaching guide for parents of CP youngsters 7 to 27 years old.

He owns Hasse Communication Counseling, LLC, which helps champions of disability employment form partnerships for win-win direct mail fundraisers.

As a Global Career Developmental Facilitator (GCDF) since 2005, he's the author of 12 Amazon eBooks, each of which explains his central premise: that disability, when framed correctly, can be a competitive advantage in today's job market for job seekers with special needs.

To access his books in electronic as well as soft-cover formats, see http://tinyurl.com/JRH-All-Books-Amazon.

Hasse developed an award-winning corporate communication function for Foremost Farms USA, Baraboo, WI, during his service of 29 years at the cooperative -- 10 of which were at the vice presidential level.

Between 1999 and 2009, he was responsible for all the online content of eSight Careers Network, New York City. As eSight's senior content developer, he wrote, assigned and edited more than 1,300 articles about disability employment issues.

Between 1997 and 2001 (before blogging became commonplace), Hasse developed, facilitated and marketed tell-us-your-story.com, a now discontinued web site where people with disabilities shared their personal-experience stories and which provided a launching pad for eSight Careers Network.

A 1965 honors graduate of the University of Wisconsin-Madison's School of Journalism, Hasse is an Accredited Business Communicator (ABC) by the International Association of Business Communicators, San Francisco, Calif.

In 1994, he received the Cooperative Spirit Award from the Cooperative Communicators Association (CCA), a national organization for professional communications employed by cooperatives, and the Cooperative Builder Award from a state-wide association of cooperatives in Wisconsin.

In 1995, he received CCA's H.E. Klinefelter Award for distinguished service in cooperative communications.

In addition to his eBooks and soft-cover books, Hasse is the author of "Break Out: Finding Freedom When You Don't Quite Fit The Mold" (Quixote Press, 1996). a memoir of 51 short stories about disability awareness.

He also compiled and edited "Perfectly Able: How to Attract and Hire Talented People with Disabilities" (AMACOM, 2011), a disability recruitment guidebook for hiring managers that highlights disability's competitive advantage in today's job market.

JIM BOOKS

7 TRANSFORMATION STORIES

Quick Career-insight Series of Seven Little Books
***for* Parents of Youngsters with CP**

Each of the seven Little Books takes about 40 minutes to read. Each illustrates and summarizes the essential career builders for your youngster's age group – all through seven transformational stories about Jim Hasse's personal experience as a person with CP.

You'll find considerably more detail about each career builder at cerebral-palsy-career-builders.com, which can be used as an ongoing reference for "how to" information as your youngster matures.

7TRANSFORMATION
STORIES

Little Book 1 (Career-coaching Series) about Self-confidence
FOR PARENTS OF ELEMENTARY STUDENTS
with Cerebral Palsy

JIM HASSE

Buy **Little Book 1** on Amazon
at- http://www.amazon.com/dp/B00DPLHRTI

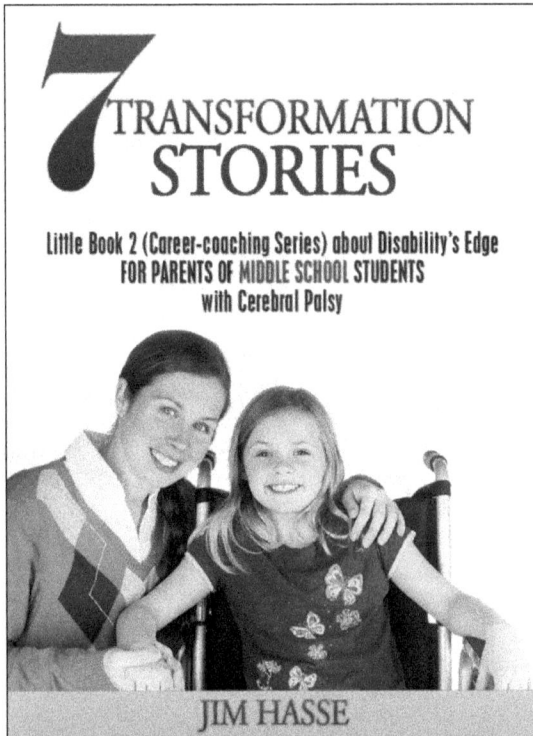

Buy **Little Book 2** on Amazon
at http://www.amazon.com/dp/B00H9WAKHA

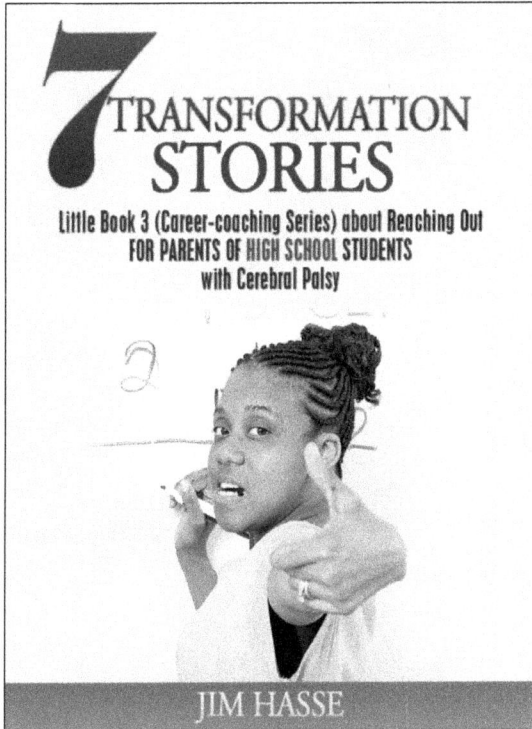

Buy **Little Book 3** on Amazon
at http://www.amazon.com/dp/B00HB77RAQ

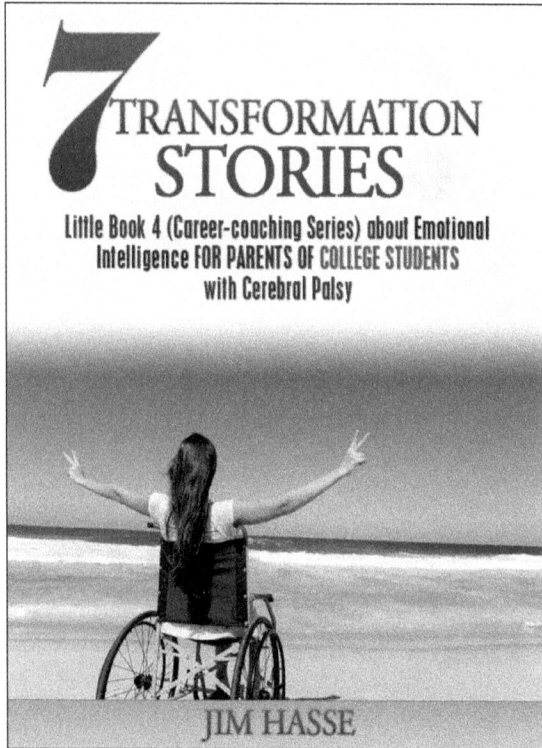

Buy **Little Book 4** on Amazon
at http://www.amazon.com/dp/B00HBDUJ96

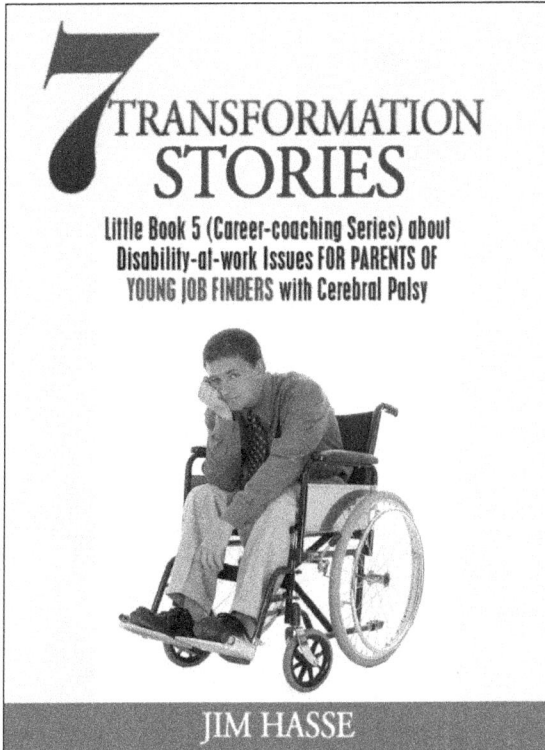

Buy **Little Book 5** on Amazon
at http://www.amazon.com/dp/B00HBVTZ02

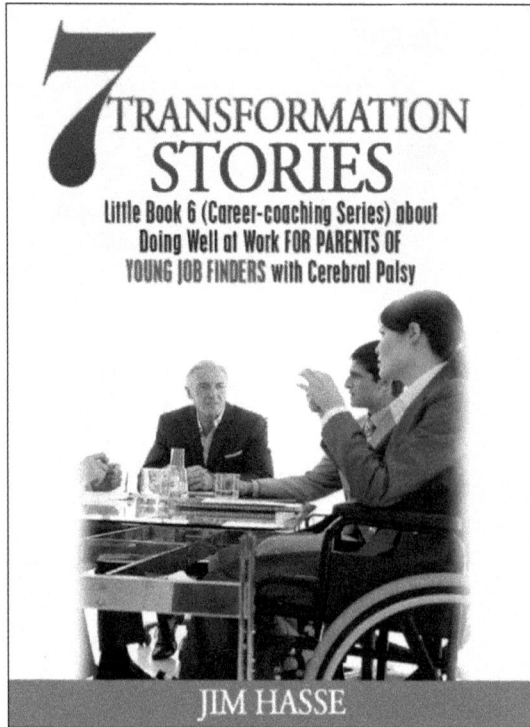

Buy **Little Book 6** on Amazon
at http://www.amazon.com/dp/B00HE60J8G

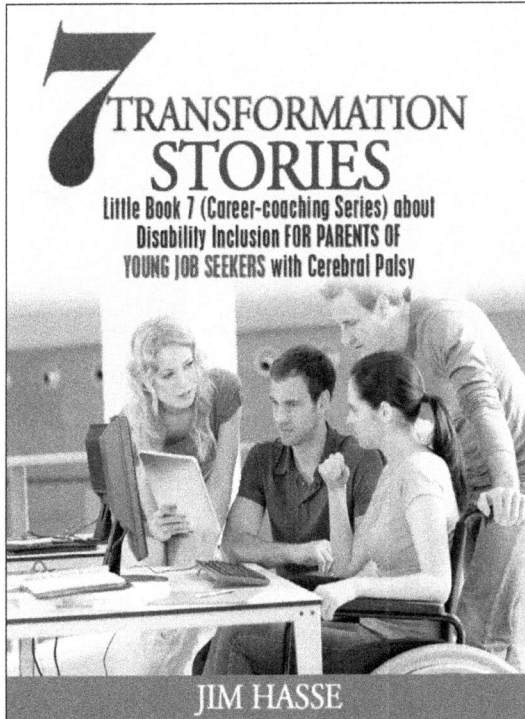

Buy **Little Book 7** on Amazon
at http://www.amazon.com/dp/B00HEVJYUU

Five Books *for* Parenting Youngsters with Special Needs

CAREER BOOK

Each of these five books (available in electronic and paperback formats) takes about 40 minutes to read. Each illustrates and summarizes the essential career development strategies to follow for your youngster's age group – all based on the roadmap recommended by National Career Development Guidelines (NCDG) and Jim Hasse's experience as a Global Career Development Facilitator and as a person with cerebral palsy and mainstream work experience.

You'll find considerably more detail about each career building strategy at www.cerebral-palsy-career-builders.com, which can be used as an ongoing reference for "how to" information as your youngster matures.

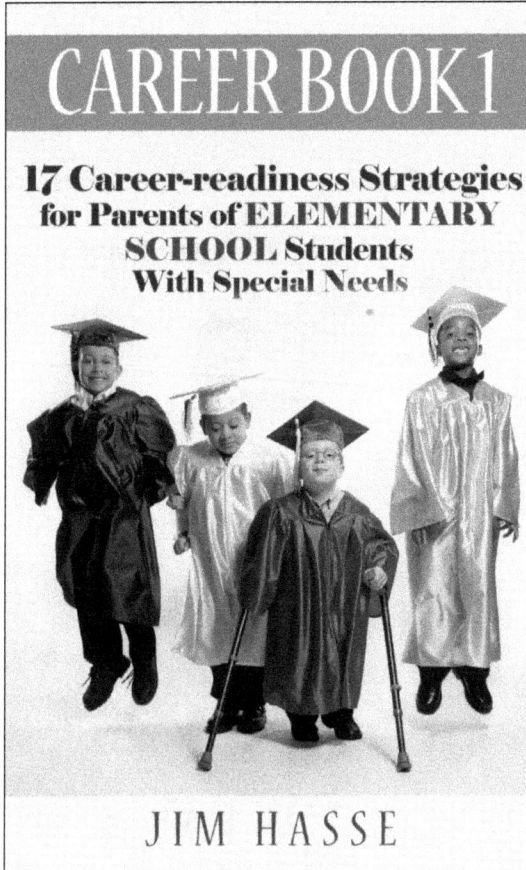

Buy **Career Book 1** on Amazon
at http://www.amazon.com/dp/B00JNYH6JM

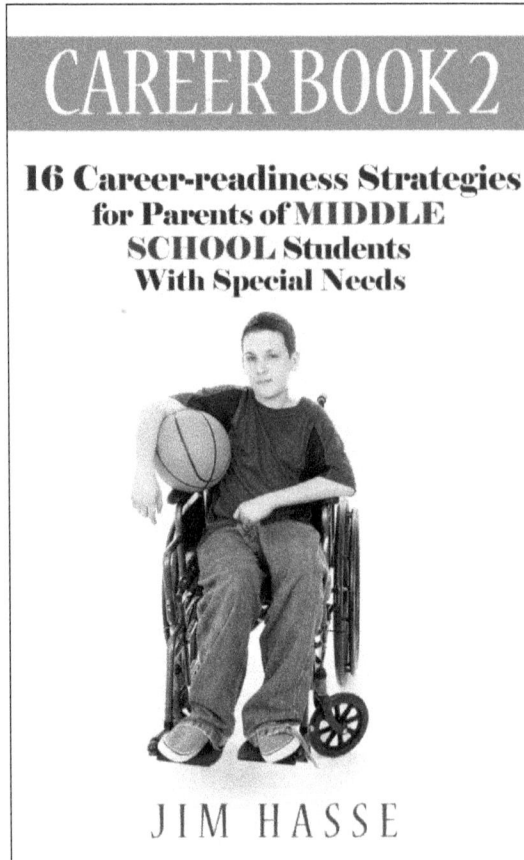

Buy **Career Book 2** on Amazon
at http://www.amazon.com/dp/B00KLIMPBS

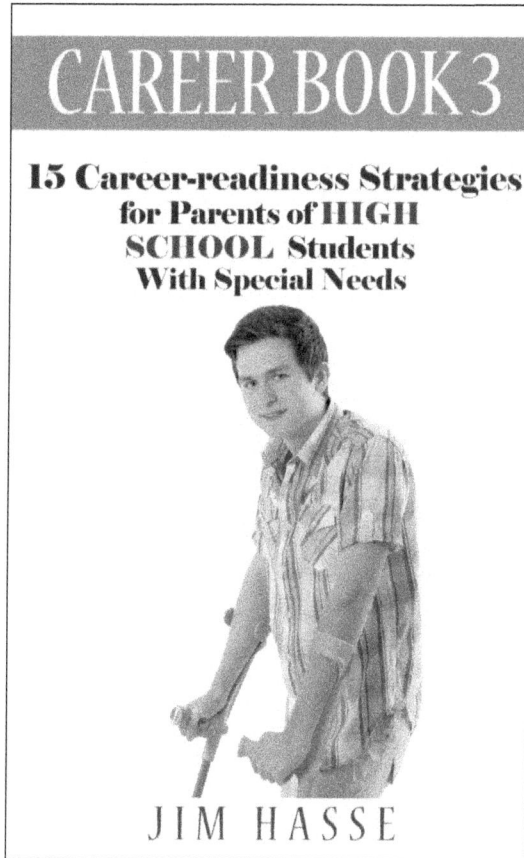

Buy **Career Book 3** on Amazon
at http://www.amazon.com/dp/B00KN2OF56

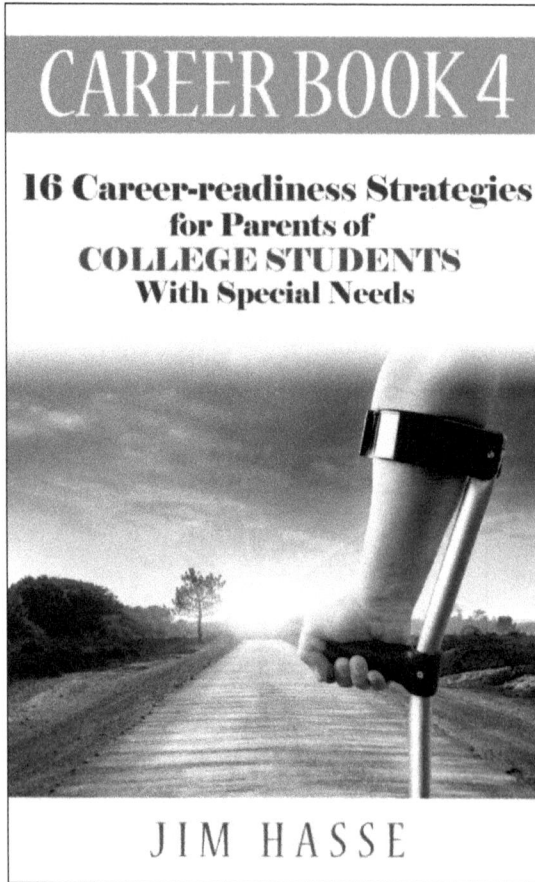

CAREER BOOK 4

16 Career-readiness Strategies
for Parents of
COLLEGE STUDENTS
With Special Needs

JIM HASSE

Buy **Career Book 4** on Amazon
at http://www.amazon.com/dp/B00KPGV5B2

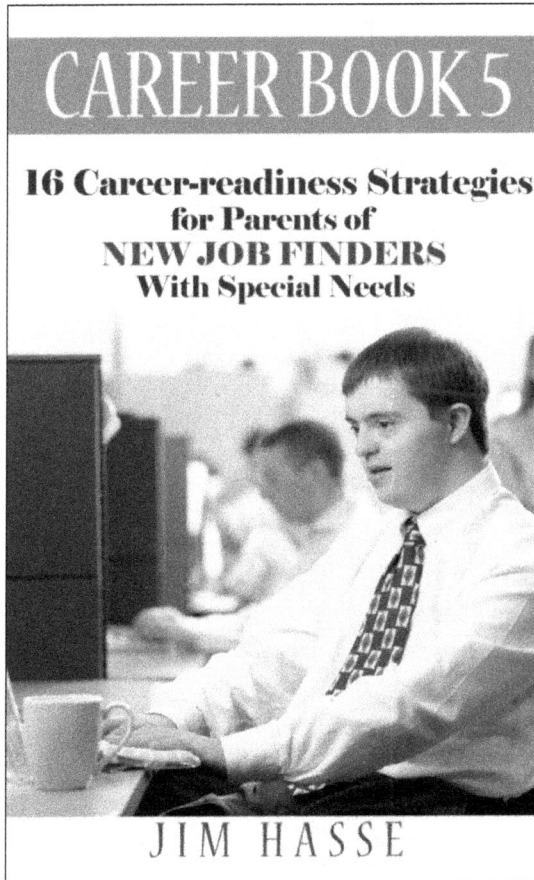

Buy **Career Book 5** on Amazon
at http://www.amazon.com/dp/B00KQRZIHC.

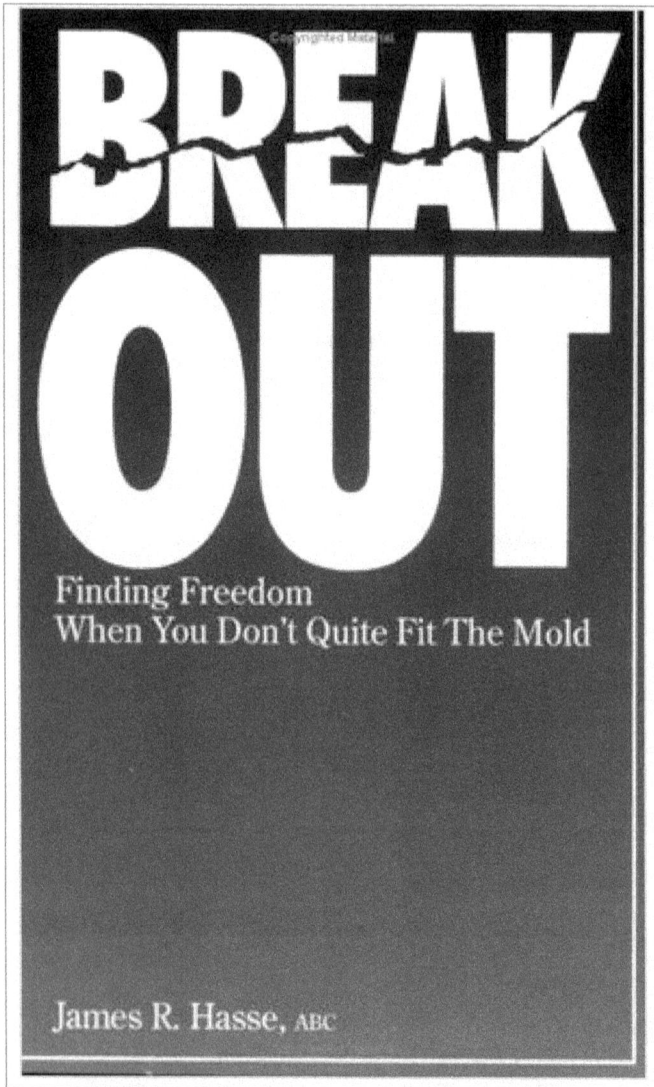

Buy on Amazon at http://tinyurl.com/breakoutjim2
"Break Out: Finding Freedom When You Don't Quite Fit the Mold,"
a memoir of 51 short stories about disability awareness (Quixote Press, 1996).

www.ingramcontent.com/pod-product-compliance
Lightning Source LLC
Chambersburg PA
CBHW060954040426
42445CB00011B/1153